2019 PISCES HOROSCOPE & ASTROLOGY

2019

Pisces

Horoscope & Astrology

Published by Mystic Shores publications

Suite SM-2380-6403

14601 North Bybee Lake Court

Portland, Oregon 97203

Phone: +1 (805) 308-6503

islandauthor@hotmail.com

Copyright © 2018 by Mystic Shores publications

Acknowledgment:

Thank you to the stargazers, dreamers, and mystics.

You make this world a better place.

2019

Pisces

Horoscope & Astrology

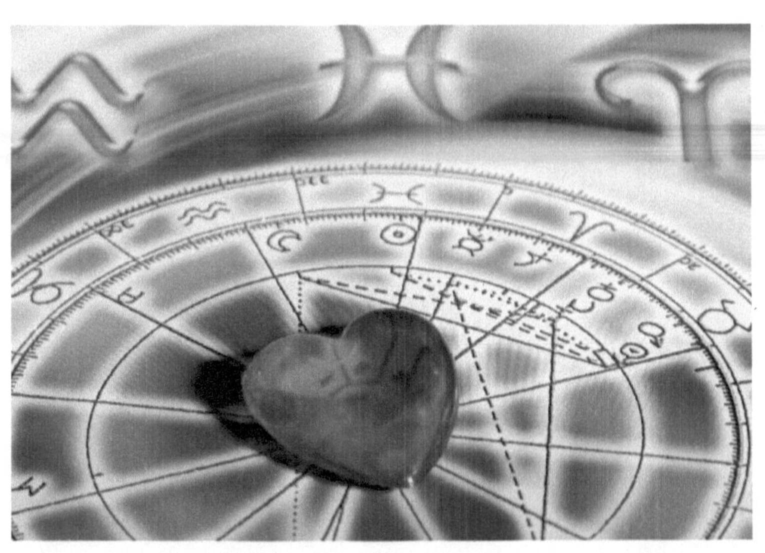

PISCES 2019 OVERVIEW

Three powerful Supermoons arrive in the first few months of 2019, this ensures plenty of dreams and secrets come into the Pisces world. This effect has an incredible ability to blend emotions with intention. The first two Supermoons are in Leo, which provides an extra boost for Pisces to distill into an interfusion which carries with it the potency of intuition and the awareness of emotions. The third Supermoon is a rare Blue Moon, and this brings mystical power for Pisces to utilize as the evolved alchemistic Pisces is. With this magic, Pisces strives to make the world a better place. To this end, Pisces is selfless, spiritual, and very focused on this idealistic journey.

There are also hurdles to navigate with Mercury Retrograde subjecting Pisces to emotional sensitivities through miscommunications with others, this can also cause unnecessary hurt in Pisces's personal relations. Knowing what to watch out for is vital, Pisces has an impressive ability to express energy which is sensitive, healing and aware. Pisces can restore lost equilibrium during these phases if mindful of the stage. Knowing about these cycles enables Pisces to regain lost ground during Mercury Retrograde phases and prevent misunderstandings from snowballing into something much more significant.

2019 is a year which blends intuition with new world idealism. This dramatically expands Pisces's Water attributes. When harnessed correctly, Pisces can make remarkable progress towards making the world a happier and more spiritually evolved place.

Pisces

Pisces Dates: February 19 to March 20
Symbol: Pair of Fish
Element: Water
Planets: Jupiter, Neptune
House: Twelfth
Colors: Purple, white

JANUARY ASTROLOGY

January 1ˢᵗ – 5ᵗʰ - Quadrantids Meteor Shower.

The Quadrantids meteor shower run yearly from January 1ˢᵗ -5ᵗʰ. The Quadrantids meteor shower peaks on the night of the 3ʳᵈ and morning of the 4ᵗʰ.

January 6ᵗʰ - New Moon in Capricorn.

This moon phase occurs at 01:28 UTC. This is an excellent time to star gaze as there is no moonlight.

January 6ᵗʰ - Venus with Greatest Western Elongation.

The planet Venus reaches it's highest eastern elongation of 47 degrees from the Sun.

January 6ᵗʰ - Partial Solar Eclipse.

This partial solar eclipse occurs in parts of eastern Asia and the northern Pacific Ocean.

January 14ᵗʰ – First Quarter Moon in Aries.

This Moon phase occurs at 06.45 UTC.

January 21st - Full Moon in Leo.

This full moon phase occurs at 05:16 UTC. This is known as the Full Wolf Moon because hungry wolf packs howled outside settlers camps. This full moon has also been identified as the Old Moon and the Moon After Yule.

January 21st - Supermoon.

This is the first of three super-moons for 2019.

January 21st - Total Lunar Eclipse.

This total lunar eclipse occurs in the majority of North America, South America, eastern Pacific Ocean, as well as the western Atlantic Ocean, extreme western Europe, and West Africa.

January 22nd - Conjunction of Venus and Jupiter.

A conjunction of Venus and Jupiter takes place with the two stunning planets within 2.4 degrees of each other in the pre-dawn sky.

January 27th – Last Quarter Moon in Scorpio.

This Moon phase occurs at 21.10 UTC.

JANUARY HOROSCOPE

JANUARY WEEK ONE

Evolution is calling your spirit towards evolving and following a higher path. While there may be some inner turmoil, you are ready to break free and expand your horizons. Your adventurous spirit is expansion orientated, and passing through a phase of healing is part of this process. A new venture has the potential to transform your world, it may shake up steadfast beliefs and expand your life towards a new perspective. You can embrace the changes which follow. Some personal and practical changes are coming into your life. This new phase is the harbinger of positive outcomes, your goals are taking you in a direction which puts you more at ease about moving out of your comfort zone. You identify areas which need development, let go of baggage which hinders progress and journey towards a time of radiant potential. This is a highly creative time which is in alignment with your higher self.

The January 6th New Moon in Capricorn has increased power to draw luck into your world.

JANUARY WEEK TWO

It is a favorable time to connect with friends, you are given the green light to embrace the social time ahead. This leads to a chapter which feels dynamic and is filled with fresh new ideas. A lively conversation with an optimistic character begins to set the stage for future progress. It may lead to a big adventure with this person, as the energy picks up steam, you visualize fun times and broad horizons. You find this is an inspiring person to be with. Soon you also find inspiring ways to become more involved in your local community. This takes you to a buoyant chapter which inspires and motivates you to connect with like-minded individuals. You experience lively communications, and it does bring a valuable sense of harmony into your surroundings. Being with your social group can facilitate healing and is restorative to your spirit.

The First Quarter Moon in Aries brings gifts, Pisceans are blessed with refreshing thoughts and innovative ideas.

JANUARY WEEK THREE

The Super Full Moon in Leo is supporting as you release past issues, these have created blockages which had been limiting your potential, being in alignment with your higher goals now allows you to head to your true calling. Staying true to your inner guidance lets you make choices which are in alignment with your emotional vision. This is especially pertinent when it comes to love, as you may have found there were difficulties which troubled your spirit in the past. Breaking free of limitations brings you positive change. Impressive results are obtained through broadening your perception, and a willingness to open your mind to a fascinating opportunity which crosses your path soon. This leads to a time which may feel unpredictable but does offer gems of potential. An adventurous spirit takes you to an exciting chapter which resonates perfectly with your rebellious tendencies. Revolutionizing and revamping your environment creates space for positive change.

Additionally, the January 21st Total Lunar Eclipse leaves Pisces feeling compassionate and spiritually oriented.

JANUARY WEEK FOUR

Venus and Jupiter conjoin this week. Sunshine enters your world soon, life becomes imbued with a powerful sense of meaning and purpose. This lightens your load considerably a sense of well-being is guiding your path towards developing an area which holds great potential to you. You appreciate the blessings which surround your situation, everything becomes more focused, clarity is highlighting the beauty which surrounds your life. News arrives to inspire personal growth. It is a beautiful time to review your options, preparation and planning become one of your personal attributes which enable incredible growth to occur. Your goals are reignited, you move forward focusing on self and identity. Ingenious plans are well received, your interests beckon, there is little to stop you, you gain traction and can finally embrace achieving a pleasing result. This lights up your sense of inspiration, the world awaits your motivated heart.

The January 27th Last Quarter Moon in Scorpio sees you take an impressive step towards achieving a humanitarian and compassionate goal.

FEBRUARY ASTROLOGY

February 4th - New Moon in Aquarius.

This Moon phase occurs at 21:03 UTC. This is an excellent time to star gaze as there is no moonlight to obscure your view of the universe.

February 12th – First Quarter Moon in Taurus.

This Moon phase occurs at 22.26 UTC.

February 19th - Full Moon in Leo.

This Moon phase occurs at 15:53 UTC. The February full moon is known as the Full Snow Moon because the heaviest snows usually fall during February. As hunting was difficult, this full moon has also been recognized as the Full Hunger Moon.

February 19th - Supermoon.

This is the second of three Supermoons for 2019. The Moon will be at its nearest approach to the Earth and will look slightly larger and brighter than usual.

February 26th – Last Quarter Moon in Sagittarius.

This Moon phase occurs at 11.28 UTC.

February 27th - Mercury at largest Eastern Elongation.

The planet Mercury reaches an eastern elongation of 18.1 degrees from the Sun.

FEBRUARY WEEK ONE

Exciting changes are indicated, this kicks off a new chapter which sees your life run to a different beat. You draw diverse characters into your world, this forms a harmonious time which enables you to embrace developing ties. It also brings you a grounded feeling which fills your tank of stability. You find life becomes more energizing, and this motivates you to keep expanding those adventurous horizons. Heightened creativity ushers in a time of change. Keep open to new opportunities, watch out for an impressive offer which provides you with the chance to restructure your environment. This brings more freedom into your surroundings and paves the way for a lively chapter which sees you network with engaging characters. You can get busy and embrace the social environment which shines a light on well-being and happiness.

FEBRUARY WEEK TWO

Some pretty significant potential is on the horizon, this reveals an opportunity which has been hidden, it can bring the raw potential to entice you to expand your horizons. It illuminates your deepest desires, attractions, and vision. It is time you reap the rewards for the efforts. Your social life picks up and brings you opportunities to engage with lively characters. Dabbling in a new area is also indicated for you. You find things begin to improve, if you've battled with low energy levels, this forward motion brings a sense of rejuvenation and restores your well-being. Taking dedicated steps to improve your circumstances enables you to apply yourself to areas which hold the highest meaning. An invitation arises, which places a focus on intimacy and joint ventures. This sweeps in with some significant changes, it takes you to an abundant horizon of potential.

FEBRUARY WEEK THREE

You enter a time of heightened intimacy and emotional bonds which are nurtured through the participation of joint ventures. It is a great time to focus on one-on-one socializing and develop a stronger connection. Additionally, there is some incredible energy coming which helps create a vision for long-term stability. Taking time to formulate a strategy for future goals begins a path towards physical realization. A karmic quality also rules this week. You are entering an emotional phase which is drawing harmony into your world. This energy paints a picture of balance, abundance, and joy. You embody thoughts, ideas, and emotions which align positively with another. It draws fantastic potential into your surroundings and does offer you the opportunity to dramatically improve your circumstances. Wearing your heart on your sleeve sees you open your heart to another soon.

FEBRUARY WEEK FOUR

It is an excellent time to clarify priorities, tweaking goals helps you get in a position to launch them successfully. There may be an opportunity for a reunion as someone from your past is likely to re-emerge. An opportunity arrives soon, which could bring exciting changes, this heralds new energy emerging to stir up your creativity and inspiration. Being able to focus your underutilized energy enables a successful result. You enter a time of personal growth and self-improvement, this takes you to new heights, you feel inspired to create change which empowers and develops your world. Long-term goals are coming into focus, strategies are designed, you come up with some big plans for future growth. An exciting offer arrives to tempt you to move in a new direction. It is a substantial time for dreaming, setting intentions, and reviewing your trajectory.

MARCH ASTROLOGY

March 5th – Mercury Retrograde begins in Pisces.

During a retrograde period, it isn't the right time to move forward in any practical venture. Be prepared for misunderstandings and miscommunications to be prevalent. You can make plans during this time, but it may be best to put them into action after the retrograde ends.

March 6th - New Moon in Pisces.

This phase occurs at 16:04 UTC. This is an excellent time to observe galaxies and stars because there is no moonlight to interfere.

March 14th – First Quarter Moon in Gemini.

This Moon phase occurs at 10.27 UTC.

March 20th - March Equinox.

The March equinox takes place at 21:58 UTC. The Sun be shining on the equator, and there will be equal amounts of day and night throughout the world. This is the first day of spring (vernal equinox) in the Northern Hemisphere.

March 21ˢᵗ - Full Moon in Libra, Supermoon.

This full Moon is on the opposite side of the Earth as the Sun and shall be adequately illuminated. This phase occurs at 01:43 UTC. This full moon is known as the Full Worm Moon because this is the time of year when the ground softens, and earthworms reappear. This full moon is also regarded as the Full Crow Moon, the Full Crust Moon, the Full Sap Moon, and the Lenten Moon. This is also the last of three super-moons for 2019.

March 28ᵗʰ – Last Quarter Moon in Capricorn.

This Moon phase occurs at 22.26 UTC. April 15 –

March 28ᵗʰ - Mercury Retrograde ends in Pisces.

You can now move forward with any delayed plans that you have been putting off due to the Mercury Retrograde phase. Relationships should soon improve as tensions ease.

MARCH WEEK ONE

Someone from your past has been looking for you, this person does plan on getting in contact with you, and it could be to a new chapter with them. This takes you to a time which highlights engaging conversations and bright ideas. It is a chapter which provides you with new inspiration and gives you the motivation to expand your horizons. You draw a sense of well-being into your life as harmony sweeps in and creates new potential. There is a situation coming in your life which allows you to explore new dynamics with another. It makes space for a closer bond and takes you to a time of happiness and harmony. Deepening the situation with someone who inspires you has a soothing effect on your spirit. It's the perfect boost to your position and lets you overhaul your personal life.

MARCH WEEK TWO

You are especially sensitive to cosmic vibrations this week, the planet Mercury went into retrograde late last week, and you begin to feel some cosmic fallout. You may have had a few intense days. This is something which has been affecting every major area of your life and requires some kind of re-calibrating for you to rejuvenate your energy. Perhaps renegotiating demands on your precious time will enable you to prioritize other areas of your life which hold significant meaning to you. As you re-balance and obtain equilibrium, tension is released, allowing more harmony to emerge in your world. This brings passion and enthusiam back. You may feel like questioning your current direction, this is to make sure that you are in alignment with your core values. Following your dreams will bring you to the correct endeavor to see your brilliance shine. You might even begin to move in a new direction soon. The important thing is, taking time to restore balance will have you feeling confident that you are on the right path.

MARCH WEEK THREE

You are current advised not to put plans into action due to Mercury retrogrades disruptive influence. You are currently in a planning phase, this is setting the stage for future progress. Reflecting about the past does give you essential insight about where to head next. You may find your priorities shifting and as you move forward with less intensity in your life, you can devote time to a pet project which captures your attention. This gives your life a touch of sparkle, it may even become one of your most cherished goals. You spend time thinking about your most profound vision and what actionable steps you need to take to get there. Your best qualities are your compassion and ability to nurture others. You can accomplish a great deal by thinking big. Expanding your horizons does spring a series of positive events into your world. You've plenty to celebrate and can embrace dedicating time towards looking after yourself this week.

MARCH WEEK FOUR

You buckle down and continue the business of planning your life expanding goals. You feel the need to plant these seeds on the solid ground. You are especially security minded, focusing on practical developments. Rewarded with tangible results, this gives you precise feedback that you are creating substantial growth in your world. This has you venture out of your standard comfort zone and expands your potential into a direction which is in alignment with your passion. You have also entered a time of self-care, nurturing and healing. This provides you with the space required to see clearly about a situation which may be confusing. Releasing old hurts adds to your reflective tone, it all heightens your ability to manifest new potential into your world. As you release and rejuvenate, you are drawn to a situation which holds plenty of enticing possibilities. Spotting this brings you a new project you can be passionate about.

APRIL ASTROLOGY

April 5th - New Moon in Aries.

This moon phase occurs at 08:51 UTC. This is an excellent time to observe galaxies and stars because there is no moonlight visible.

April 11th - Mercury at most substantial Western Elongation.

The planet Mercury reaches its most substantial western elongation of 27.7 degrees from the Sun.

April 12th – First Quarter Moon in Cancer.

This Moon phase occurs at 19.06 UTC.

April 19th - Full Moon in Libra.

The Moon is on the opposite side of the Earth as the Sun and will be completely illuminated. This moon phase occurs at 11:12 UTC. This full moon is known as Full Pink Moon because it marks the appearance of the first spring flowers. This full moon has also been identified as the Sprouting Grass Moon, the Growing Moon, and the Egg Moon. Many coastal areas call it Full Fish Moon because this was the time the fish swam upriver to breed.

April 22nd, 23rd - Lyrids Meteor Shower.

The Lyrids meteor shower runs each year from April 16-25. This meteor shower peaks on the night of the 22nd and the morning of the 23rd. These meteors sometimes produce bright dust trails that last for several seconds.

April 26th – Last Quarter Moon in Aquarius.

This Moon phase occurs at 22.18 UTC.

APRIL WEEK ONE

It is an extensive time for you as you embark on a new chapter. Change is likely to sashay into your world. As you venture down a path towards the realization of your dreams, you reflect on the journey you have been on recently. You reinvent your potential and become bold about obtaining your needs and assert yourself which increases your confidence tenfold. This is highly attractive to others and encourages bold and exciting moments into your life. An opportunity arises soon which brings out new friends and fresh starts to your life. A capable, caring, and enticing person may also arrive in your world. They are willing to explore developing a closer connection with you. This enables you to feel blessed with close friendships, and meaningful activities. You enjoy light-hearted fun with those who are close to you. Deep conversations flow over into useful areas of your life.

APRIL WEEK TWO

You enter a phase which is especially poignant. This enables you to reflect on the past and achieve inner guidance which helps propel you forward towards the realization of your dreams. Fine tuning your vision does put the focus on drawing harmony into your life. You enter a growth orientated chapter which sees a boost come your romantic life. This is guiding you to transform your life as change is in the air. There does seem to be a restructuring taking place, and this sees you evaluating a future vision and looking at improving your personal happiness. There is a sense that you have reached the end of a chapter and evolution or change is indicated. This leads you towards a situation which is more settled, and it does draw more happiness into your personal life. The move could be a new aspect in your current romantic situation or see you seeking an entirely new involvement.

APRIL WEEK THREE

The Full Moon in Libra makes a stunning appearance to inspire and motivate you this week. You have the power to change your life and can embrace a joyful event soon. You possess excellent organizational skills, and an opportunity emerges soon which enables you to put them to good use. A new venture inspires you creatively and brings you in contact with other innovative characters. Expanding your social set brings further opportunities for lively discussions and social outings which bring you a sense of abundance and well-being. This is a fortuitous time which brings new people into your life for a reason. Expect an extensive time which is focused on developing an area of your life which holds significant meaning. This enables you to move forward suddenly and excitingly. This sweeps away regret and doubt and helps you build your life in a way which suits your current goals. Your tender emotions are influencing these changes, this can feel impulsive, spontaneous, and even rebellious. The changes ahead move towards a more authentic phase of life.

APRIL WEEK FOUR

You are capable and enterprising able to learn from the past and utilize these lessons in your daily life. This sees you enter a productive time which is highly creative with nature. Intentions set are likely to unfold in a way which draws happiness into your life. A cherished dream is the heart of this phase. You turn your attention to an area which is especially crucial and think big about taking the steps necessary to make it happen. You shift towards expansion and engage with the broader world. There are events on the horizon which allow you to meet some new exciting people and seek out new areas to develop. You are on a path of growth and learning, and this takes you towards developing some significant goals. As your vision widens you see a variety of options to tempt you towards change. News arrives, which provide you with a welcome boost.

MAY ASTROLOGY

May 4ᵗʰ - New Moon in Taurus.

This phase occurs at 22:46 UTC. The new moon phase is a brilliant time to observe galaxies and stars because there is no moonlight visible.

May 6ᵗʰ, 7ᵗʰ - Eta Aquarids Meteor Shower.

The Eta Aquarids meteor shower runs annually from April 19 to May 28. It peaks this year on the night of May 6 and the morning of the May 7.

May 12ᵗʰ – First Quarter Moon in Leo.

This Moon phase occurs at 01.12 UTC.

May 18ᵗʰ - Full Moon in Scorpio, Blue Moon.

The Moon is on the opposite side of the Earth as the Sun, and its face will be fully illuminated. This phase occurs at 21:11 UTC. The May full moon is known as the Full Flower Moon because this is when spring flowers are in abundance. This full moon is also known as the Full Corn Planting Moon and the Milk Moon. This year it is also a blue moon. This unusual calendar event only happens once every few years, giving rise to the term, "once in a blue moon." There are usually three full moons in each season. A fourth full moon is called a Blue moon and occurs on average once every 2.7 years.

May 26th – Last Quarter Moon in Aquarius.

This Moon phase occurs at 16.33 UTC.

MAY HOROSCOPE

MAY WEEK ONE

Your attitude is bright and optimistic, this helps you tune in with a new area to develop. Setting intentions enables you to create a path towards adventure. You enter a time which involves an impromptu get-together or social celebration. Stoking those embers brings you a sense of well-being. Spending time with your closest friends is especially nurturing and restores balance. You may even form a close alliance with a kindred spirit soon. Focusing on the areas of self and identity allows your vitality to return. This revives your energy and can help you focus on your personal goals. Putting your dreams up front helps create a sense of excitement and possibility. Tangible results are obtained through perseverance and a willingness to be flexible.

MAY WEEK TWO

The influence of your heritage is especially strong for you this week. This provides you with a pioneering sense of creativity. You are sensitive and emotionally aware. While this can be difficult for you at times, it also takes you towards authentic expressions and meaningful bonds. The more you nurture the ties that bind, the higher the positive effect which ripples through your life. It is a time which emphasizes developing an area which holds meaning to you. The most prominent aspect is the healing that takes place as you release outworn situations. Moving towards a happier chapter has been a strong theme for you, and you continue to stay true to your authentic self this week. An intimate conversation provides you with fresh information, this lightens your mood and inspires you to think about your future prospects.

MAY WEEK THREE

A rare Blue Full Moon occurs in Scorpio this week. You have intuitive abilities which you have inherited. This is a gift which can be difficult for you to understand, especially when you doubt your skills. You can deepen your talents through focused attention, and practice. A chance to put this into action is likely to present itself soon. Just give it your best shot, you will likely feel drawn to the correct direction. This expands your horizons and allows you to be in tune with your higher self. You are entering a time of transformation, as you focus on yourself you move into alignment with a path which reflects your current needs. This sees circumstances improving in your romantic situation. You are likely to feel at a crossroads, unsure which way to take, but a positive sign will help guide you towards the direction which develops your personal life, it enables you to blaze beautifully forward towards finding your happiness.

MAY WEEK FOUR

An opportunity arrives soon which may feel tantalizing, it begins with a discussion which comes out of the blue and brings on a sense of excitement. You may think that you're not ready for significant development, yet you are grateful for this chance to improve your learning curve. You will get the correct result if you focus on each step of the process. Maintaining a positive attitude ensures there are plenty of positive new beginnings. You have visionary abilities. Continue to nurture your talents, and you will soon see signs that help guide your path. You may receive an invitation which creates space for innovative expression, this self-development helps soothe frazzled nerves and generally enables you to progress. Stay open to opportunities which seek to enter your life, as you are ready to transform. This is a time of building stable foundations and creating robust growth.

JUNE ASTROLOGY

June 3rd - New Moon in Gemini.

This moon phase occurs at 10:02 UTC. This is an excellent time to observe galaxies and stars because there is no moonlight to interfere.

June 10t – First Quarter Moon in Virgo.

This Moon phase occurs at 05.59 UTC.

June 10th - Jupiter at Opposition.

The planet Jupiter will be at its nearest approach to Earth, and its planet face will be illuminated entirely by the Sun.

June 17th - Full Moon in Sagittarius.

The Full Moon is on the opposite side of the Earth as the Sun, and its face will be completely illuminated. This moon phase occurs at 08:31 UTC. This full moon is known as Full Strawberry Moon because it is the peak of strawberry harvesting season. The June Full Moon has also been identified as the Full Rose Moon and the Full Honey Moon.

June 21ˢᵗ - June Solstice.

The June solstice occurs at 15:54 UTC. The North Pole will be tilted toward the Sun, which, having reached its northernmost position in the sky will be over the Tropic of Cancer at 23.44 degrees north latitude. This heralds the first day of summer (summer solstice) in the Northern Hemisphere, and is considered one of the most influential times of the year for many traditional cultures.

June 23ʳᵈ - Mercury at largest Eastern Elongation.

The planet Mercury reaches most substantial eastern elongation of 25.2 degrees from the Sun.

June 25ᵗʰ – Last Quarter Moon in Aries.

This Moon phase occurs at 09.46 UTC.

JUNE HOROSCOPE

JUNE WEEK ONE

This is a time of nurturing yourself and enjoying the simple pleasures of life. Your horizons will likely broaden over the coming weeks. Honoring your emotions will enable you to stay open when a particularly important moment blesses your path soon. You are entering a time of intensity which sheds light on your highest goals. You feel ready to embark on a new journey, departing from your usual sense of security, you make way for a broader understanding of change. You have reached a time of transformation and are ready to embrace the changes ahead. You open your heart and become more expressive than usual, this is a sign that you are prepared to make the most of every day and focus on planting positive energy. What's more, you are also likely to work on the building blocks of your career life which leads to a new chapter emerging. As you push past barriers, you head forward towards the realization of goals.

JUNE WEEK TWO

The planet Jupiter reaches its closest approach to the earth this week. The planet Jupiter rules luck and growth. New opportunities are set to emerge, and this plants the seeds for you to explore new horizons. A significant progressive moment provides you with insight that is a stroke of genius. This heightens your goal orientated abilities, as it is in alignment with an area that is ripe for development. You have plenty of motivation to begin a new direction, and this inspires you to open the steps of developing your life in positive ways which bring you joy. This is a fruitful time for emotional processing and soul-searching. You are entering a time of transformation, and it is imperative that you focus on your needs and shed any unnecessary baggage. Doing this inner work illuminates a new area which becomes the foundation for your next phase. You are being guided to listen to your intuition and head towards your passions. This is pushing you towards growth and adventure.

JUNE WEEK THREE

This is the perfect time to focus on nurturing yourself. Enjoying self-care lightens your spirit considerably, there are heightened opportunities for networking and friendships ahead. As you experience an increase in social gatherings with friends and colleagues, you can relax and rejuvenate your spirit. This will re-balance and restore harmony to the next phase which has you getting back to your trailblazing and innovative self. This is a great time to forge ahead with new connections and collaborations. Your wild spirit embraces the expansion which occurs over the coming weeks. You meet original people and innovative thinkers. It's a beautiful time to connect with your tribe and mingle. You can expect a lively social activity soon which has you feeling excited and inspired.

JUNE WEEK FOUR

You gain insight into someone who captivates your awareness. This can be a difficult journey at times as you don't always see eye to eye with this person. They are perceptive and intuitive, and this can feel oppressive if the energy isn't grounded correctly. You may find you need to re-balance your thoughts and spend time in moments, gathering your emotional resources. The more you think about how to best develop your goals, the easier the path becomes, as there is an insight to be gained which leads to progress being made. This is not the easiest of roads, but the rewards are robust if you are brave of heart and willing to take a long-term approach. The more you focus on obtaining a high result, the better your prospects become. It is a path which requires dedication and perseverance but pays off in the end with beautiful rewards.

January 1ˢᵗ – 5ᵗʰ - Quadrantids Meteor Shower.

July 2ⁿᵈ - New Moon in Cancer.

This moon phase occurs at 19:16 UTC. This is an excellent time to observe galaxies and stars because there is no moonlight visible.

July 2ⁿᵈ - Total Solar Eclipse.

The total solar eclipse occurs in parts of the southern Pacific Ocean, central Chile, and central Argentina. A partial eclipse is visible in the Pacific Ocean and western South America.

July 7ᵗʰ – Mercury Retrograde begins in Leo.

During a retrograde period, it isn't the right time to move forward in any practical venture. Be prepared for misunderstandings and miscommunications to be prevalent.

July 9ᵗʰ – First Quarter Moon in Libra.

This Moon phase occurs at 10.55 UTC.

July 9th - Saturn at Opposition.

The beautiful ringed planet Saturn will be at its nearest approach to Earth, and it will be illuminated by the Sun.

July 16th - Full Moon in Capricorn.

The July Full Moon is located on the opposite side of the Earth as the Sun and will be fully illuminated. This phase occurs at 21:38 UTC. This full moon is known as Full Buck Moon because the male buck deer start to grow new antlers. This full moon is also known as the Full Thunder Moon and the Full Hay Moon.

July 16th - Partial Lunar Eclipse.

The partial lunar eclipse will be visible throughout most of Europe, Africa, central Asia, and the Indian Ocean.

July 25th – Last Quarter Moon in Taurus.

This Moon phase occurs at 01.18 UTC.

July 28th, 29th - Delta Aquarids Meteor Shower.

The Delta Aquarids meteor shower peaks on the night of July 28 and morning of July 29.

July 31ˢᵗ - Mercury Retrograde ends in Cancer.

You can now move forward with any delayed plans
that you have been putting off due to the Mercury
Retrograde phase. Relationships should soon
improve as tensions ease.

JULY HOROSCOPE

JULY WEEK ONE

You have many talents which will emerge over the coming months. As a matter of fact, you can expect an upgrade to your circle of friends. Meeting someone, you feel a close connection with providing you with plenty to celebrate. You've taken plenty of hard knocks in life, but now can reshape your life and rebuild your potential. This relates to having gone through a life transition which forced you to mature young. You are now going through another important change which takes you to new levels of personal responsibility. Now you are ready to take on the world. Boosts to your self-sufficiency allow you to achieve new heights of potential. It is the perfect time to channel your energy toward something tangible and career building. Expect news to arrive which speaks of an invitation out. This leads to a happy occasion and sets the stage for future progress.

JULY WEEK TWO

Life has taught you some problematic lessons, and you could benefit from opening up new horizons. Devoting yourself to a path which resonates with you on a deeper level would be beneficial and healing. Your emotions and most profound parts of your spirit reveal a wealth of creativity which seeks to emerge. Communications are likely which allow you to find an emotional resolution, this is regarding a recent upsetting situation which has led to feelings of disappointment and betrayal. Acknowledging what has occurred helps take your focus towards channeling your restless energy constructively. Healing helps quiet down your anxious heart. Some vital progress is around the corner which will provide valuable answers for you. This is a mindful opportunity for personal growth and reflection. Contemplation leads to a personal break-though.

JULY WEEK THREE

There will be an opportunity coming soon which will be the perfect occasion to venture out with your tribe. You find yourself expressing affection with someone you have a long history with. Sunlight shines upon the development of bonds with this person. This allows stable foundations to provide you with a sense that the energy you share is grounded and holds many blessings. Feelings of warmth and abundance surround you. You are heading towards a larger cycle of personal evolution, this could see big news arrive. As you mix your creativity with this potential, you may find yourself drawn to developing a closer bond with a kindred spirit. This leads to a time of expansion and optimism. It helps you seek new horizons and ride a wave of hopefulness towards a future destination. As you renew faith in the process, abundance flows into your world.

JULY WEEK FOUR

Fantastic opportunities are likely which involve personal growth and launching towards a new area which inspires you. It is a great time to embark on new endeavors as you have an unusual amount of inspiration set to arrive. Exploring new activities provide you with engaging social encounters. You shine a light on your core self and emotional needs during a moment of introspection. Let your feelings guide your progress and embrace nurturing your world. Wonderful changes are indicated. This really pushes you to get things moving in the right direction. It leads to a harmonious time, and significant developments are possible in your personal life. This centers around compromise and equality, it allows things to last over the long haul. The deepening of bonds with another give you a heartening glimpse of what may be possible as you go deeper down this road. The manifestation of loving relationships is likely.

AUGUST ASTROLOGY

August 1ˢᵗ - New Moon in Leo.

This moon phase occurs at 03:12 UTC. This is an excellent time to observe galaxies and stars because there is no moonlight to interfere.

August 7ᵗʰ – First Quarter Moon in Scorpio.

This Moon phase occurs at 17.31 UTC.

August 9ᵗʰ - Mercury at most substantial Western Elongation.

The planet Mercury reaches greatest western elongation of 19.0 degrees from the Sun.

August 12ᵗʰ, 13ᵗʰ - Perseids Meteor Shower.

The Perseids meteor shower runs each year from July 17 to August 24. It peaks this year on the night of August 12 and the morning of August 13.

August 15ᵗʰ - Full Moon in Aquarius.

The August Full Moon is located on the opposite side of the Earth as the Sun and will be fully illuminated. This phase occurs at 12:30 UTC. The August full moon is known as the Full Sturgeon Moon because sturgeon fish of the Great Lakes and other major lakes are plentiful. This full moon has also been identified as the Green Corn Moon and the Grain Moon.

August 23rd – Last Quarter Moon in Taurus.

This Moon phase occurs at 14.56 UTC.

August 30 - New Moon in Virgo.

This moon phase occurs at 10:37 UTC. This is an excellent time to view galaxies and stars because there is no moonlight to interfere.

AUGUST HOROSCOPE

AUGUST WEEK ONE

You could soon be the recipient of some exciting news. An illuminating conversation provides you with insight which helps your personal goals and projects move forward at a faster pace. A sense of a reawakening takes place, and you bust through limitations to arrive at heightened creativity. It's the perfect time to map exciting plans and formulate goals with a stable structure. There could soon be a boon to your social life. This touches your emotional side and leaves you especially motivated as it dramatically inspires you to keep expanding your horizons. This burst of positive energy really rockets you forward into a new area which brings you joy. It evokes beautiful moments and may lead to a significant breakthrough. Keeping your heart open enables this positive energy to flow in. This is a happy time which sees your circumstances improve as harmony increases.

AUGUST WEEK TWO

You may be feeling restless and edgy lately, this is guiding you to express yourself transparently to others in your life who love you dearly but may be overprotective of you. You have a desire to expand your horizons and try new adventures. Take a deep breath and plunge towards your dreams. You are being supported by the universe to achieve your goals, you are being drawn in two different directions. One area is urging you to head towards growth and adventure, the other area is looking back at the past. At times it might feel like you take one step forward, two steps back. You will find the right balance between moving forward, as well as staying true to the past. Prioritizing your self-development leads to dreaming and pragmatic planning, it is the perfect way to turn your visionary ideas into reality. You may feel some sadness at this time, but ultimately it paves the way for a new chapter of potential, once you release the baggage of the past.

AUGUST WEEK THREE

You may face difficulties ahead and need to face your fears to overcome limitations. You have the power of regeneration urges you to take time to nourish and support yourself and those around you and release painful emotions which arise. It is time to make a firm stance against a situation which has occurred. You express your person viewpoints with honesty and openness. You nail opposition with tenacity and daring. Additionally, an extra workload could also drain your energy as you take on many responsibilities. It is essential to take time to focus on self-care, re-balancing your energy and being firm with others helps to establish barriers. You may find an intriguing offer of collaboration also arrives to inspire you to take an offer of assistance. Sharing the load smooths over any rough edges which could otherwise occur over the next few weeks.

AUGUST WEEK FOUR

This is a difficult time, and you may feel as though every significant area of your life is shifting, which can be both thrilling and exhausting. As this intense energy is having a grand effect on you, you may feel its intensity peak at crucial times. This could bring issues swiftly to the forefront and destabilize your energy. Spending time on relaxing activities enables you to re-balance and restore your core foundations. Your workload may be increasing and causing you to feel drained. There is one area which is causing you consternation, and you are having to carefully check your options, you will feel the solution intuitively, bringing your life back into balance. Clarity is obtained through careful reflection and by looking at the big picture, at what is most important to you on a fundamental level. Once you identify the essential element, go for it.

SEPTEMBER ASTROLOGY

September 9ᵗʰ - Neptune at Opposition.

The giant blue planet will be at its closest approach to Earth, and its face will be illuminated by the Sun.

September 6ᵗʰ – First Quarter Moon in Sagittarius.

This Moon phase occurs at 03.10 UTC.

September 14ᵗʰ - Full Moon in Pisces.

The September full Moon is on the opposite side of the Earth as the Sun, and its face will be fully illuminated. This phase occurs at 04:34 UTC. This full moon is known as the Full Corn Moon because the corn is harvested around this time. This full moon is also called the Harvest Moon which is the full moon that occurs nearest to the September equinox each year.

September 22ⁿᵈ – Last Quarter Moon in Gemini.

This Moon phase occurs at 02.41 UTC.

September 23ʳᵈ - September Equinox.

The 2019 September equinox occurs at 07:50 UTC. The Sun shines directly on the equator, creating equal amounts of day and night throughout the world. This is also the first day of fall (autumnal equinox) in the northern hemisphere and is considered a significant zodiac event for many cultures.

September 28th - New Moon in Virgo.

This phase occurs at 18:26 UTC. This is an excellent time to observe galaxies and stars because there is no moonlight visible.

SEPTEMBER WEEK ONE

You to expand your talents into a new area. A form of creative self-expression may be of interest to you and lead you down a new path. As you become in touch with your creative side, you explore a new passion which could lead to a beautiful chapter of potential, it may even bring you in contact with like-minded individuals who encourage your efforts and entice you to go out and about more often. You reveal an opportunity to learn more about yourself and an individual you meet soon. It is an event which offers support and encouragement. Giving your all to this opportunity sees the situation become more open, friendly, and singles may find it even leads to intimacy. The closeness you achieve with this character could unfold over time if you can keep nurturing the potential possible. You will soon likely receive news which brings a sense of excitement. It takes a few steps to get up to speed, there is plenty of potential connected to this development. Expect communication which brings new beginnings.

SEPTEMBER WEEK TWO

The planet Neptune is at its closest approach to Earth this week, it will be at its brightest. The planet Neptune rules the areas of dreams and healing. You have faced difficulties in the past, which have had you call on your inner warrior to overcome hurdles and meet the future with a resilient heart. You can now make incredible strides in drawing harmony into your world. There is an emphasis placed on spiritual connections which help expand your social circle. Sweeping changes are indicated which give you a sense of making substantial strides toward your reaching goals. You have made great tracks on your personal journey all told this year. This sees you continue to evolve towards achieving significant growth and greater stability. A stream of creativity flows through your world encouraging you towards greater self-expression and allowing you to indulge your instincts in new endeavors. An impromptu social event also provides you with a memorable time and sets the stage for a future get-together. It is a bodacious chapter for networking.

SEPTEMBER WEEK THREE

A more positive vibe enters your life soon. This encourages you to map out a plan for future progress, your goals are colorful, creative, and vibrant. This is leading you towards a time of heightened self-expression where you follow your passions and embrace the emotional energy which seeks to emerge. You are likely to form a collaboration with a friend soon who inspires you to dream big. You receive recognition for a complicated venture you have been working on. This gives you the valuable feedback needed to continue to work towards the achievement of goals. An opportunity crosses your path which intrigues you, but you are not sure if it will be too complicated, taking time to clear your mind will resolve any doubts and provide you with a clear direction to move towards. You meet someone who inspires your outlook and brings you happy times. You love lively discussions and can look forward to impressive social outings which fill your life with laughter, and positive thinking. This is a week which resonates abundance and joy.

SEPTEMBER WEEK FOUR

The Equinox this week indicates growth opportunities arriving soon. There are some positive changes noted which see you developing your talents and getting excited about an ambitious venture which emerges to inspire your creativity. As your personal perspective broadens you embrace the brilliance which reveals your overall progress. This time is highly organized, you highlight areas which need working on and find the resources to create positive change. You turn a corner, become proactive about fine-tuning prospects. Your life is set to head towards an upswing in the form of higher potential and opportunity. You see increases which inspire your motivation, this is a sign of positive reinforcement that you are making the correct changes needed to achieve success. You may be nearing the completion of what has been a frustrating time in your life. Now you see the light at the end of the tunnel and can embrace the changes which herald in a new chapter of potential.

OCTOBER ASTROLOGY

October 8th - Draconids Meteor Shower.

The Draconids meteor shower runs annually from October 6-10 and peaks this year on the night of the 8th.

October 5th – First Quarter Moon in Capricorn.

This Moon phase occurs at 16.47 UTC.

October 13th - Full Moon in Aries.

The October full Moon is on the opposite side of the Earth as the Sun, and its face will be fully illuminated. This phase occurs at 21:09 UTC. This full moon is known as the Hunters Moon because at this time of year the leaves are falling, and game animals are plentiful. This full moon is also known as the Travel Moon and the Blood Moon.

October 20th - Mercury at Greatest Eastern Elongation.

The planet Mercury reaches greatest eastern elongation of 24.6 degrees from the Sun.

October 21ˢᵗ - Last Quarter Moon in Cancer.

This Moon phase occurs at 12.39 UTC.

October 21ˢᵗ, 22ⁿᵈ - Orionids Meteor Shower.

The Orionids meteor shower runs yearly from October 2 to November 7. Orionids meteor shower peaks this year on the night of October 21 and the morning of October 22.

October 27ᵗʰ - Uranus at Opposition.

The planet Uranus will be at its nearest approach to Earth, and its face will be illuminated by the Sun.

October 28ᵗʰ - New Moon in Scorpio.

This moon phase occurs at 03:39 UTC. This is an excellent time of the month to view galaxies and stars because there is no moonlight visible.

October 31ˢᵗ – Mercury Retrograde begins in Scorpio.

During a retrograde period, it isn't the right time to move forward in any practical venture. Be prepared for misunderstandings and miscommunications to be prevalent.

OCTOBER HOROSCOPE

OCTOBER WEEK ONE

You may feel extra sensitive during the time ahead, this takes you to a sentimental and nostalgic chapter. It shines a light on your closest bonds, especially those that are nearest and dearest. Turning your attention to these most intimate ties does inspire you to focus on the area of home and family. It marks a turning point which draws the essence of abundance into your world. This time heralds an essential chapter of expanding opportunity and sees you dive towards personal goals. New horizons beckon and tempt you towards a fresh episode of potential. Meeting a kindred spirit and sharing communications enable you to spread your wings. This is a perfect time to team up and blend ideas. It brings exciting news to you and plants the seeds that blossom over the coming phase. Making strides in your personal life provides a sense of joy and well-being.

OCTOBER WEEK TWO

You are set to benefit from a favorable time which has you feeling independent yet connected to those close to you. You are exceptionally creative and able to harness your talents towards an ambitious endeavor. Basically, this brings real interests into your world. You may find personal goals are also energized as you are motivated to complete unfinished projects. Fresh own plans and dreams are coming into your life. This takes you to an expansive chapter which opens you to a myriad of possibilities which await your unique gifts. You are ready to feel upbeat and embrace new potential. An opportunity to be involved in a group activity looks promising and leads to a joyous time with kindred spirits. It is an enchanting time to deepen bonds.

OCTOBER WEEK THREE

An opportunity emerges which gives you something to work towards. It provides you with validation that you are the right path. You make many discoveries of this kind, and as you learn, you find the lessons learned reveal more potential which can be expanded upon. This all has a stunning effect on your outlook and takes you to a new and happier chapter. Newfound wisdom leads you on a dance of personal discovery and enlightenment. You tend to take things to heart and feel anxiety and doubt, you can now learn from past difficulties, and apply what you've learned to achieve beneficial outcomes. Seeking a new way to do things will give you the best chance of dealing with things. An opportunity coming up in the days ahead, take time to think it through, it looks perfect for you. This is a direction which sees you face fear and move toward new goals.

The planet Uranus will be at its closest approach to Earth this week. The planet Uranus rules change and originality. You focus on new ideas and are inspired to begin developing a venture which holds promise. This is an inspiring time which sees you enter a fresh chapter of potential. Sharing your thoughts with another enables you to blend ideas and discuss how best to develop the potential which is tempting you towards personal growth. You know you want to create a solid path forward. Using insight and planning for the future provides you with a blueprint you can use. It is a path of learning and wisdom. New information is likely to help give you guidance. Staying flexible allows you to adjust course as needed and obtain the highest result on this path. You can achieve your vision, setting solid intentions enables things to shift towards the achievement of goals. You are prepared to work to arrive at your chosen destination.

NOVEMBER ASTROLOGY

November 4ᵗʰ – First Quarter Moon in Aquarius.

This Moon phase occurs at 10.23 UTC.

November 5ᵗʰ, 6ᵗʰ - Taurids Meteor Shower.

The Taurids meteor shower runs yearly from September 7 to December 10. It peaks this year on the night of November 5.

November 11ᵗʰ - Rare Transit of the planet Mercury Across the Sun.

The planet Mercury moves directly between the Earth and the Sun. This is a rare event that occurs only once every few years. The next transit of Mercury does not take place until 2039.

November 12ᵗʰ - Full Moon in Taurus.

The November full Moon is on the opposite side of the Earth as the Sun, and its face will be fully illuminated. This phase occurs at 13:36 UTC. This full moon is known as Full Beaver Moon as this was the time of year beaver traps were used. It is also known as the Frosty Moon and the Hunter's Moon.

November 17th, 18th - Leonids Meteor Shower.

The Leonids meteor shower runs yearly from November 6-30. The Leonids meteor shower peaks this year on the night of the 17th and morning of the 18th.

November 19th – Last Quarter Moon in Leo.

This Moon phase occurs at 21.11 UTC.

November 20th - Mercury Retrograde ends in Scorpio.

You can now move forward with any delayed plans that you have been putting off due to the Mercury Retrograde phase. Relationships should soon improve as tensions ease.

November 24th - Conjunction of Venus and Jupiter.

A conjunction of Venus and Jupiter is visible on November 24. The two planets are within 1.4 degrees of each other in the night sky.

November 26th - New Moon in Scorpio.

This phase occurs at 15:06 UTC. This is an excellent time to view galaxies and star clusters because there is no moonlight visible.

November 28th - Mercury at Greatest Western Elongation.

The planet Mercury obtains western peak elongation of 20.1 degrees from the Sun.

NOVEMBER WEEK ONE

It is a beneficial week ahead which ensures you embrace life. You break free from constraints, and an unusual level of freedom emerges. A current endeavor is highlighted and will likely be detail orientated. It could involve an overhaul of a project you have been doing or considering. It is a beautiful time for reconnecting with your aspirations and allowing the sun to shine on your life. It's an exciting and inspiring time for you. Opportunities are likely which help you revamp your identity. You may even decide to change your whole approach to life. This indicates a personal transformation. It may catapult your creativity to new heights. You will likely become more assertive and confident, this is magnetizing to others, it conveys the message that you are someone who knows what you want in life. You are original, innovative, and have a flair for self-expression this week.

NOVEMBER WEEK TWO

This week the planet Mercury makes a rare transit across the Sun. As it moves between the Sun and the Earth, it fires up consciousness, and you sweep away that which no longer serves you. You are in a phase of expansion which is connected to your subconscious. This provides you with many options, and it is an excellent time to step out of your comfort zone. Set your intentions and adopt a new proactive perspective. The winds of inspiration are ready to carry you to new levels of success. Your motivation will be especially important, and this will help you achieve your goal. As you negotiate the path ahead, you maintain balance and transform. There are specific opportunities ahead which lead you towards sunny skies. You are ready for expansion and optimism. New experiences call your name and encourage you to broaden your horizons. Study, learning, and growth are indicated, and this could be the beginning of an enlightening phase for you. You meet someone who inspires your imagination, this person is adventurous, intuitive, and insightful. They bring out a brighter, lighter side to life.

NOVEMBER WEEK THREE

This week teems with a vibrant world of potential, you feel inspired to share your passion with others, and this enables new experiences to entice you out of your usual routine. There are times which provide you with valuable lessons, staying true to your core values gives you with a path that leads to abundance. A need for self-improvement manifests in opportunities to develop your lifestyle. You reawaken to the potential possible. A windfall of potential arrives to inspire you to create new areas of interest. You buckle down and focus on achieving a high result. Focusing on your priorities provides you with ample opportunities to shine. Seeds are planted during an intimate conversation which blossoms further down the line. Overall this week, communication and your social life are on an upward trend. You may even score a new kindred spirit to bond with.

NOVEMBER WEEK FOUR

You can expect opportunities ahead which enable you to make the most of your innovative linking. Be prepared to take calculated risks, you can be optimistic and roll out big ideas for development. If you feel the excitement and high energy currently surrounding you, this is a positive sign you are on the right track. You can expect your social circle to expand as you are entering a highly expressive phase which reveals potential ripe for the taking. This directly relates to achieving goals, gaining prosperity and rewards. You are steadfast, reliable, and secure. You complete the finish of a creative undertaking and be ready to begin a new journey. As you gather your harvest, you can enjoy the success of your labors. This week involves a time of celebration and excitement, you may feel invigorated by success, and can begin to plan your next chapter.

DECEMBER ASTROLOGY

December 4th – First Quarter Moon in Pisces.

This Moon phase occurs at 06.58 UTC.

December 12th - Full Moon in Gemini.

The Moon is on the opposite side of the Earth as the Sun, and its face will be fully illuminated. This moon phase occurs at 05:14 UTC. This full moon is known as the Full Cold Moon because this is when chilly winters air arrives and nights become long and dark. This full moon is also known as the Long Nights Moon and the Moon Before Yule.

December 13th, 14th - Geminids Meteor Shower.

The Geminids meteor shower runs each year from December 7-17. The Geminids meteor showers peaks this year on the night of the 13th and morning of the 14th.

December 19th – Last Quarter Moon in Virgo.

This Moon phase occurs at 04.57 UTC.

December 22ⁿᵈ - December Solstice.

The 2019 December solstice occurs at 04:19 UTC. The South Pole of the earth tilts toward the Sun, which, having reached its most southern place in the sky, is directly over the Tropic of Capricorn at 23.44 degrees south latitude. This December solstice also marks the first day of winter (winter solstice) in the Northern Hemisphere.

December 21ˢᵗ, 22ⁿᵈ - Ursids Meteor Shower.

The Ursids meteor shower occurs each year from December 17 - 25. This meteor event peaks this year on the night of the 21st and morning of the 22nd.

December 26ᵗʰ - New Moon in Capricorn.

This moon phase occurs at 05:15 UTC. This is an excellent time to view galaxies and stars because there is no moonlight visible.

December 26ᵗʰ - Annular Solar Eclipse.

An annular solar eclipse occurs because the Moon is too far away from the Earth to adequately hide the Sun. This results in a ring of light around the dark Moon. The Sun's corona is not visible during an annular eclipse.

DECEMBER WEEK ONE

This is an expansive month which puts you in the mood to socialize and collaborate with like-minded individuals. You enter a community-driven phase, which expands your life through getting involved with teamwork and cooperative ventures. A newfound sense of belonging has a healing effect, and you tap into a visionary cause which inspires your spirit. Overall, this is a bustling week with heightened productivity as a driving force behind it. Your social environment heads towards group orientated activities which provide you with opportunities to connect with like-minded individuals. You feel secure and able to mingle, opening yourself up to connecting with others. This leads to an enticing chapter which allows you to make a splash and enjoy heightened social opportunities. This entire season illuminates a fabulous month of passion, glamour, and creativity for you to embrace.

DECEMBER WEEK TWO

This is a positive chapter for personal growth. An exciting moment arrives, which shines a light on the area of relationships. You transition towards new potential. Closing the door on situations which are toxic brings an exciting phase of possibility and creativity into your world. A social event entices you to spend time with an individual who is intelligent and insightful. This person holds the key to heightened potential. An offer arrives to set the tone for the rest of this month. December shimmers with possibility and opportunity. A goal you are working towards takes shape, and valuable feedback enables you to refine your efforts. You make a conscious effort to distance yourself from energy vampires and people who drain your spirit. This allows you to reach the heights of productivity. It is a favorable time which fuels and motivates you to push ahead and achieve a high result.

DECEMBER WEEK THREE

You will soon have a powerful reminder of how far you have come and where you're hoping to go. Don't be afraid to put your own needs on the front burner as this puts you in touch with some cherished projects and goals. It's time to look at your own vision and find a path which is in alignment with your personal desires. You see a balance between giving to others and caring for your individual needs. You can expect to notice a sense of serendipity, and in these sweet moments, you will feel joyful and happy. You open your heart to embracing happiness and move towards a phase of fulfillment. Spending time with your closest ties sends a signal to enter a time of rejuvenation and healing. Your spirit is rebooted and this is so cleansing for your soul. A lively moment ahead sees fun and laughter bring joy into your world. This is the icing on the cake and brings a wonderful feeling of festivity into your life.

DECEMBER WEEK FOUR

Your social circle expands, everything proceeds in a direction which feels correct. Romantic energy is particularly potent as someone is thinking about sharing their deeper feelings with you. They are especially touched by your presence, this brings up intense emotions which have them wanting to move out of their comfort zone as scary as that seems to them. They are hoping to stop staying in limbo, let down their guard and become vulnerable with you. Not everything unfolds at once, but a meeting of minds occurs soon, which eclipses anything you have previously experienced. This is a communication driven chapter which enables you to express your ideas and develop a meaningful bond with another. Harmony governs your world, you engage in lively conversations which drive a closer situation forward. This gets you in touch with a lifestyle which you can feel enthusiastic about. You spend time planning future goals and a sense of excitement eclipses any doubt you may have held about being bold and daring. The future is ripe fo the taking, and your brave heart holds the key to future happiness.

Dear Reader,

I hope you have enjoyed planning your year with the stars utilizing Astrology and Zodiac influences. Twelve zodiac star sign books are released each year which detail a monthly list of astrological events, and a weekly (four weeks to a month) horoscope. You can find me on my Facebook page:

https://www.facebook.com/SiaSands

Feedback is welcomed and appreciated.

Many Blessings,

Sia Sands

www.ingramcontent.com/pod-product-compliance
Lightning Source LLC
Chambersburg PA
CBHW031146250726
48655CB00002B/855